Sip & Paint with Happiness

DIY Paint Party at Home

For Teens and Adults

Six African-Inspired Paintings
with Simple Tutorials for
Your Home Sip & Paint Parties

HAPPINESS AKANIRO

*God is love & love brings happiness
Thanks for creating happiness with me!*

Happiness Akaniro
2/26/17

Contents

About The Author	4
What You Need to Know	5
Art Is a Stress Reliever	6
What You Need to Get Ahead of Party Day	7
What You Need to Remember About Painting	10
About Acrylics	10
Caring For Your Brushes	10
How to Prepare a Grid Canvas	12
Painting Tutorials:	13
Glorious Beauty—Acrylic on Canvas	14
Hot Stepper—Acrylic on Canvas	19
Lady at the Bar—Acrylic on Canvas	22
African Sculpture I—Acrylic on Canvas	26
African Peacock—Acrylic on Canvas	31
Conclusion	42

Copyright © 2017 by Happiness Akaniro. All rights reserved.

SIP & PAINT at Home

Do-It-Yourself Paint Party
with Happiness

....

Dear Host,
Drinks and food. This is totally up to you. Typically, finger foods or Super Bowl–style snacks and/or appetizers are good enough, but, ultimately, it depends on the kind of party you're planning and other factors like your preference, guests' preferences, etc. So, we will leave that to you. When it comes to drinks, also know that just because you're hosting a sip and paint event, you do not have to serve alcohol. You can provide whatever refreshments you want and/or ask your guests to BYOB (bring your own bottle.) Any other non-alcoholic refreshment or beverage of your choice is good enough (I think).

Dear Guest,
If alcohol is provided, please know your limit, be aware of alcohol consumption rules and age restrictions in your area, and please don't drink if you must drive.

This here is the last time I'll be too serious about giving instructions in this book. Hey, it's supposed to be fun.

Why Sip and Paint?
Any reason you can think of to bring people together for a celebration or to network is reason enough for a paint party. Be it birthdays, bridal showers, just hanging out, team building, fundraisers and the likes, or just being home alone and wondering how to pass your time. So grab your brushes, grab your glasses, and let's sip and paint with Happiness!

About The Author

Happiness Akaniro is a professional artist who lives in New Jersey. She was born in Nigeria and later migrated to United States where she earned her Master of Fine Arts degree. Happiness loves to teach and is passionate about art. She has a fun and loving personality that is infectious and reflected in her work.

Happiness hosts *Sip and Paint with Happiness* paint parties for private and public events. Happiness is also author of *Women in African Print Fashion Adult Coloring Book* an African-inspired coloring book published 2016.

Visit **www.happinexx.com or www.sipandpainthappiness.com** for more information, ideas and paint party resources.

What You Need to Know

Now that you've made that decision to paint, here is something you really need to know: Painting is relaxing. Let your strokes flow freely, and you'll gently ease yourself into a peaceful state.

You need to enjoy the process, enjoy every single brush stroke and every single mistake. In fact, there's no mistake in painting unless you say so. If it looks like an error to you, don't fret. I don't see mistakes when I paint; I see possibilities and use them to a creative advantage. You know what? This should be your defense right here. You're permitted to use that last sentence whenever your friends try to critique your painting, and if you master that line, they'll buy it. Hey, what can you do? If you were sipping while painting, anything can happen, and weird strokes do happen and are permitted in painting. So, let nobody stress you out.

You know what else? See that "error" as the mark of a moment in time. Consider it a unique mark that you may never achieve again. "Once bitten, twice shy," they say, even in the field of painting. Think of a painting error as you might some other problem in "real" life: let it be a reminder of a time when you weren't so concerned about being perfect, a time when you let things happen without trying to control every single aspect of a situation. See the potential in mistakes, and either go over them with another try or ignore them. But enjoy them. Never ever stress mistakes, or that worry might turn on you and make you feel bad about creating in the first place.

Now I'm asking myself, How did I transition from giving a lesson on painting to talking about life? It happens. Sometimes art imitates life and vice versa. I guess one can actually learn a lot about life from painting. The summary of this all—in the end, if your painting doesn't turn out exactly as you hoped it would, appreciate it for what it has turned out to be—a totally new painting! It's the effort that counts, and the joy you get from doing this activity. Without intending to, though inspired by my painting, you may have created a masterpiece that no one else but you could have created. The only one of it's kind in town. Enjoy!

Art Is a Stress Reliever

Painting is one of those activities that can help you relax. You can do it alone or in a group while having fun, laughing, and being social. It's also amazing how even when in a group setting each individual can still be transported into a peaceful state of relaxation, forgetting all worries. Sometimes, though, one or two persons may not want to let you be at peace. So I composed a mantra to send a message to potential distractors. This should be said out loud by all before painting activities begin in order to ward off any distractors. (It might work, but I can't guarantee anything!)

> Relax
> don't judge me
> and don't stress me
> when I paint for fun
> my brush is like a wand
> it takes the stress away
> and makes me feel real good
> and if you
> take it's place
> I'll make you go away
> so be good
> say I'm good
> and let us have some fun

What You Need to Get Ahead of Party Day

Canvas:
12 x 16 (recommended) or 16 x 20 inches canvas or board. If the canvas or board is primed, make sure it's primed with acrylic gesso and is not an oily surface.
A bigger canvas will take too much table space. You don't want your guest fighting over table space.

Acrylic Paint:
Acrylic paints are preferred, because they are not as messy as oil paints, and they dry very fast. Your guests are guaranteed to take a dry painting home with them same day or night depending on when you like your party.

Brushes:
For each guest, one large-size bristle brush, flat or round, for painting over large areas. One medium-size bristle brush, round tip—this will be used the most. Sometimes I see people creating their paintings using only these two brushes, a large and a small. I don't know how they do it, but they do, and they are happy with the results. So, according to people who I've sipped and painted with, you can use two brushes—if you're not worried about details like we professional artists are. I guess, as an artist, I have over-trained eyes, and maybe that is why I just have to use a third brush.
Get a third brush if you're concerned about details. Small round bristle round tip for fine details. I recommend 2 or 3 brushes for each guest. I intentionally didn't mention brush sizes not to scare you, but if you are particular, get brush number 8, 4 and 2.

Pencils: For sketching the beginning layout.

Water:
A single container of water is good. A big container for rinsing your brushes. I use big party cups, but any other sturdy cup will do.

Rag or paper towel:
For wiping paint off your brush before rinsing, so that your water doesn't get murky too quickly.

Easel:
If you have one, great. If not, you can place your canvas flat on the table. If you don't have easels available, please use the smaller 12 x 16 canvas for easier handling. The bigger canvas will take too much table space. You don't want your guests fighting over table real estate.

Paper Plates:
Paper plates are good alternative for mixing palettes. They are inexpensive and disposable. Large ones give you enough room to mix your colors if you want to.

Aprons:
Disposable plastic or paper aprons; cloth aprons also work.

Get what you can and remember, this is supposed to be fun. So, you're going to make the best of what you have, or in some cases, what you don't have.
Most of the materials for creating this painting can be bought at any art or craft store. Take note that these materials come in different brands and have varying price tags, and most of the time the prices are based on whether they are professional or student-grade. Student-grade materials can be good enough. Remember, a DIY sip and paint party is just for the fun of it, but your painting may turn out to be so good that you'll want to have a whole separate art show around it. It can happen! Anything can happen when people party and paint.

List:
1. Canvas: 12 x 16 inches (recommended)
2. Acrylic Paint: Various colors depending on the painting you pick for your event
3. Brushes: At least one large (flat or round) and one medium size
4. Pencils
5. Water: Cup of water for each guest
6. Rag or Paper Towel
7. Easel: You can place the canvas on a table, if you don't have easels, but easels are ideal.
8. Paper Plates
9. Aprons

10. The Drinks and Food: This is totally up to you. Typically, finger foods or Super Bowl–style snacks and/or appetizers are good enough.

11. Make your grocery list...
12. Remember to invite your friends

If you don't want to be bothered with sketching in objects or prefer to only paint using already drawn art, check my website **www.sipandpainthappiness.com** for ideas and some unique pre-drawn canvas selection.

What You Need to Remember About Painting

Painting is relaxing. It's the effort that counts and the joy you get from doing this activity. Though inspired by one of my paintings, your painting is yours. Your very own creation. Own it! So, relax and enjoy your party.

While painting don't eat your paint or drink from your painting cup. On TV, artist are found of holding brushes in their mouth. Don't emulate them. There are also tales of people who accidently reached for their painting cup instead of wine glass. So, be careful. Host, make sure the cups are easily identifiable.

Make sure any previously used brush is left in the cup of water to keep it from drying. Also be careful not to smear paint on furniture as your host might not invite you back. Do not pile on the colors onto your plate at once. Take a little at a time and go back for more if you need more.

About Acrylics

Acrylics are water based medium and the way to get the best of acrylic is to make sure your brush is not dry but always moistened with water (not dripping wet) to help the acrylic flow better on your canvas surface. If you think you have too much water on your brush, dab with a paper towel, load more paint and spread on your canvas area using back and forth stroke. If the area isn't covered at first, leave to sit for a little, when it's dry you can add another layer. In about two hours or less, depending on how thick your paint layer and how big your canvas area, your painting should be dry and ready to take home with you.

Caring For Your Brushes

When you're done painting, rinse your brush with cold or lukewarm water. With your fingers massage the paint off the bristles, you can use hand soap if you want. After rinsing, place them upright in a cup or jar - bristle end up.

Some of the paintings in this book were created using a lined canvas known as a grid canvas; others do not require a lined canvas. If you prefer not to line your canvas, you will still be able to follow the steps and will achieve similar results.

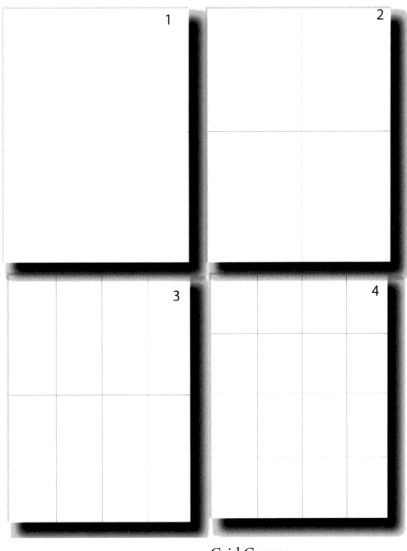

Grid Canvas

How to Prepare a Grid Canvas

This step is optional. You can skip the grid lines and draw freehand if you feel you can.

Doing a rough sketch of the object we intend to paint helps a lot. It makes the painting process easier and saves you the time in the long run, because you'll have established the outlines and boundaries right from the beginning, and then you'll be able to focus on just filling in the colors.

In some tutorials, a line drawing of part of the subject to be painted on a 12 x 16 canvas is included. You can make a copy of the drawing and cut out the shape which you can then use to trace out the beginning profiles.

Start by dividing up your canvas area with pencil lines that will serve as guide marks. Identify the halfway points on each side of the canvas, and connect the lines from one end through the center of the canvas to the opposite side, creating four sections. Then run lines through the fist half and the second half, and repeat one more time until you have sectioned up your canvas as shown.

Following here are beautiful paintings you can create in less than two to three hours.

Painting Tutorials:

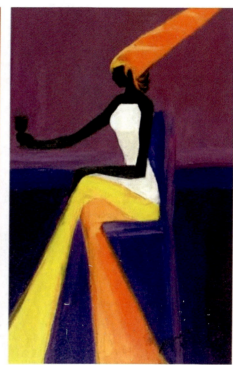

GLORIOUS BEAUTY—ACRYLIC ON CANVAS

Colors: red, yellow, white, black, yellow ochre, purple
or
cadmium red, cadmium yellow, titanium white,
lamp black, yellow ochre, purple lake

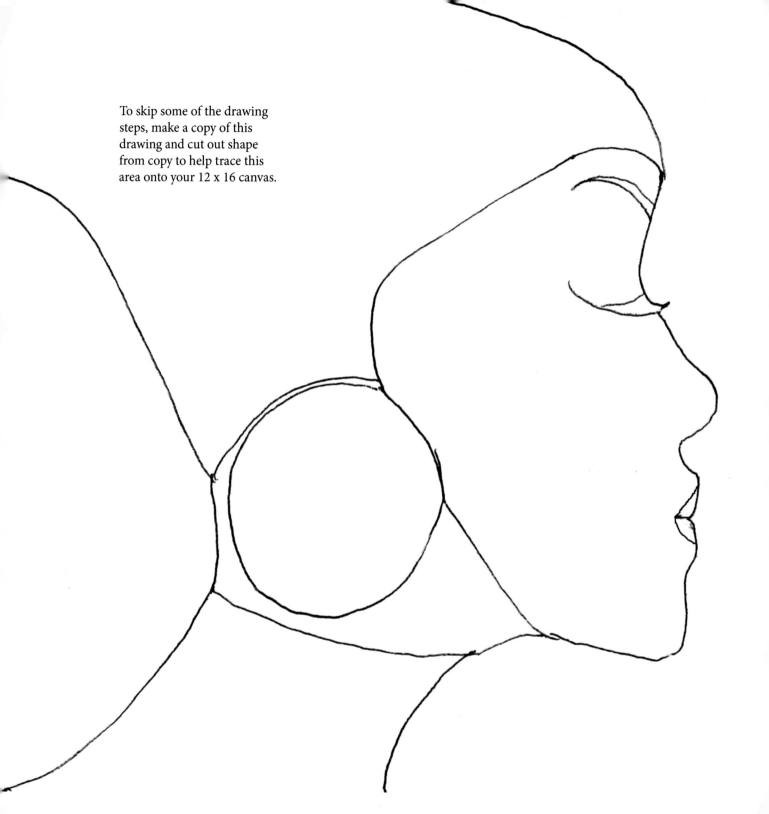

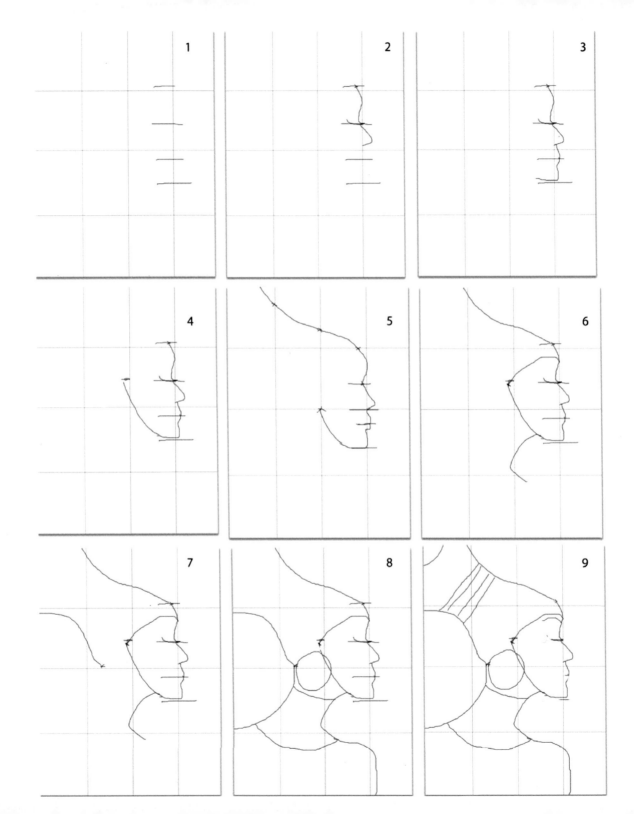

Colors Used:

 Red

 Yellow

 White

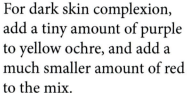 Black

For dark skin complexion, add a tiny amount of purple to yellow ochre, and add a much smaller amount of red to the mix.

For darker skin tone, continue to add tiny amounts of purple till the desired shade is achieved.

For lighter skin tone, mix yellow ochre and white, add small amount of yellow and a touch of red.

Dark skin tone: Yellow ochre or mustard + purple + red =

Lighter skin tone: Yellow ochre or mustard + white + yellow + red =

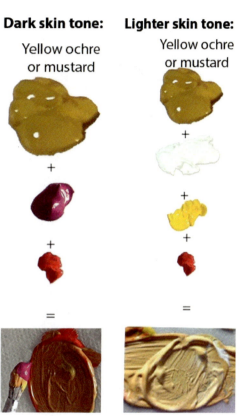

How to Paint:
Using a medium sized brush, apply color of choice to the canvas. Spread the paint on desired areas using back-and-forth brush strokes. Use the large brush to fill in the background.

Your colors don't have to match the original painting. Feel free to use your own choice of colors, and be open to accidental discoveries.

After applying the first layer of color, you may go over the area with another coat of paint, if you like.

Painting Steps:

HOT STEPPER—ACRYLIC ON CANVAS

Colors: black, blue, white, green, purple, red
or
lamp black, ultramarine blue, titanium white, viridian green, purple lake, cadmium red

Colors Used:

Black
Blue
White
Green
Purple
Red

Start by roughly drawing your figure, using a medium sized brush. Block out areas with color. Your colors don't have to match the original painting. Be open to accidental discoveries Use the large brush to fill in the background.

After applying the first layer of color, you may go over the paint with another coat, if you like, but don't overdo it, and don't force it to perfectly match my painting. There's really no perfect painting; the imperfections are a great part of what makes your artwork your own, so make it yours.

The background streaks are a mix of red and purple. You achieve the streak effect by painting with a brush loaded with two different colors at the same time. Do not try to mix the colors into each other on your plate or palette, but apply the brush to the canvas with the two fresh colors sitting side by side on your brush. Then, using
back-and-forth strokes, apply the paint to the canvas, allowing some happy accidents to happen. Don't force it; let it happen.

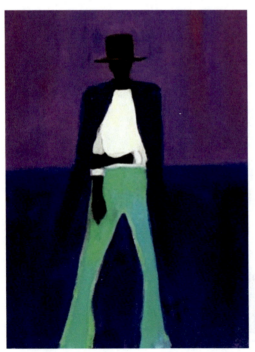

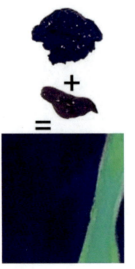
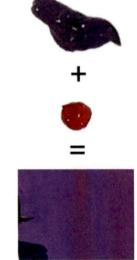

Painting Steps:

21

LADY AT THE BAR—ACRYLIC ON CANVAS

Colors: purple, red, orange, yellow, black, white, blue
or
purple lake, cadmium red, cadmium orange, cadmium yellow, lamp black, titanium white, ultramarine blue

Colors Used:

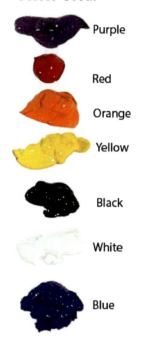

- Purple
- Red
- Orange
- Yellow
- Black
- White
- Blue

Like in the previous painting, start by roughly sketching in your figure with a medium brush.

After applying the first layer of color, you may go over the figure with another coat of color.

The upper half of the background is mostly purple. Add white to purple to achieve lighter shades.

To achieve the yellow and orange color mix effect on her pants, paint with a brush loaded with two different colors at the same time—orange and yellow. Do not try to mix the colors into each other on your plate or palette, but apply the brush to the canvas with the two fresh colors sitting side by side on your brush. Then, using back-and-forth strokes, apply the paint to the canvas while you allow some happy accidents to happen.

Painting Steps

A good idea is to leave the tiny details till last because while painting in the background, the details always get covered somehow. So, do the background and other areas, then leave the details like nose for last or even choose to go without details. Nothing wrong with that.

African Sculpture I—Acrylic on Canvas

Colors: blue, dark green, light green, white, yellow, orange, red
or
ultramarine blue, viridian green, emerald green, cadmium yellow, cadmium orange, cadmium red

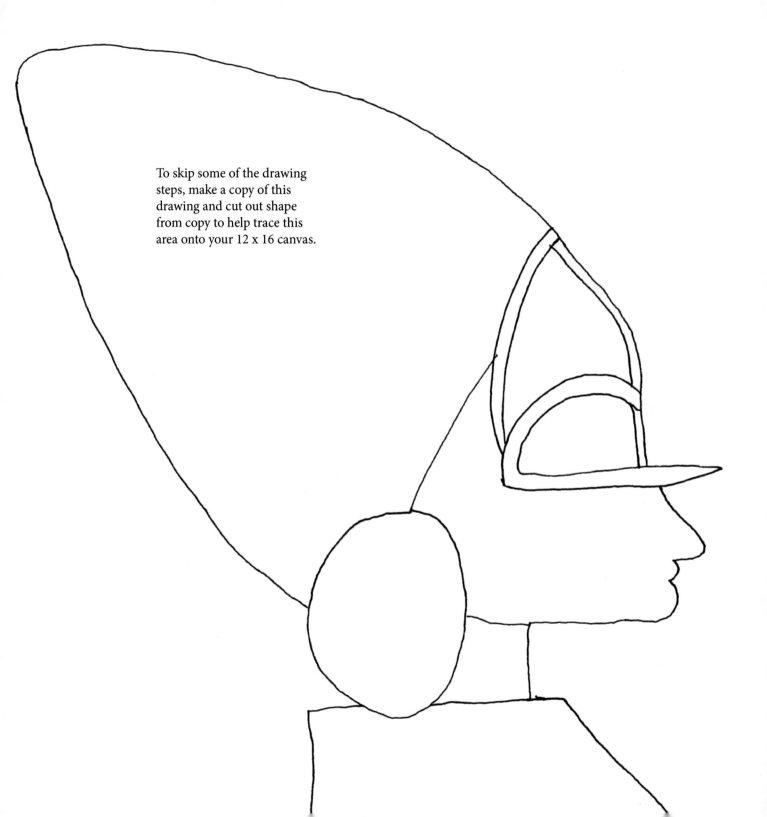

Colors Used:

Grid canvas is used in this tutorial. Follow the instruction for how to prepare a grid canvas (see page 11), sketch free hand, use the template drawing on previous page or skip the grid, and go straight to painting.

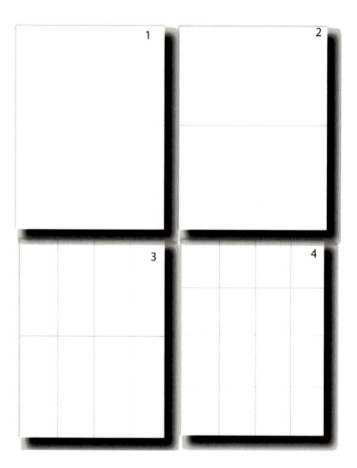

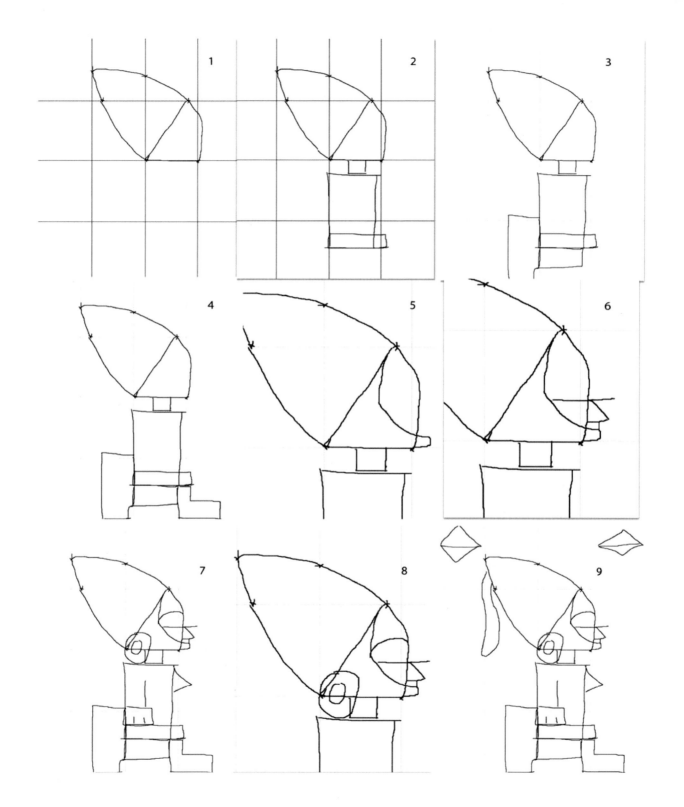

Painting Steps:

AFRICAN PEACOCK—ACRYLIC ON CANVAS

Colors: blue, dark green, light green, white, yellow, orange, red, black
or
ultramarine blue, viridian green, emerald green, titanium white, cadmium yellow, cadmium orange, cadmium red, lamp black

Colors Used:

- Blue
- dark green
- light green
- white
- yellow
- orange
- red
- black

Grid canvas is used in this tutorial, follow the instructions on how to prepare a grid canvas. You may decide to skip the lines and go straignt to drawing freehand or totally skip all these and go straight to painting.

Do your best getting the lines in if you decide to, but also remember that the drawing is temporary. You'll cover it up with paint as you continue. So, don't stress it.

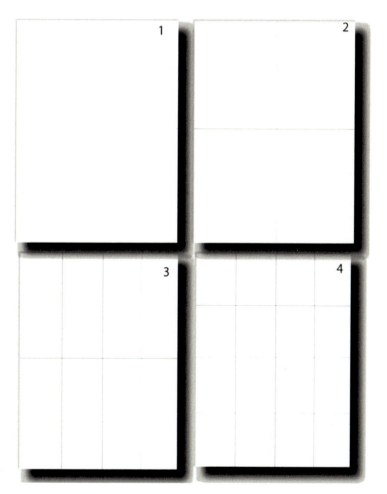

33

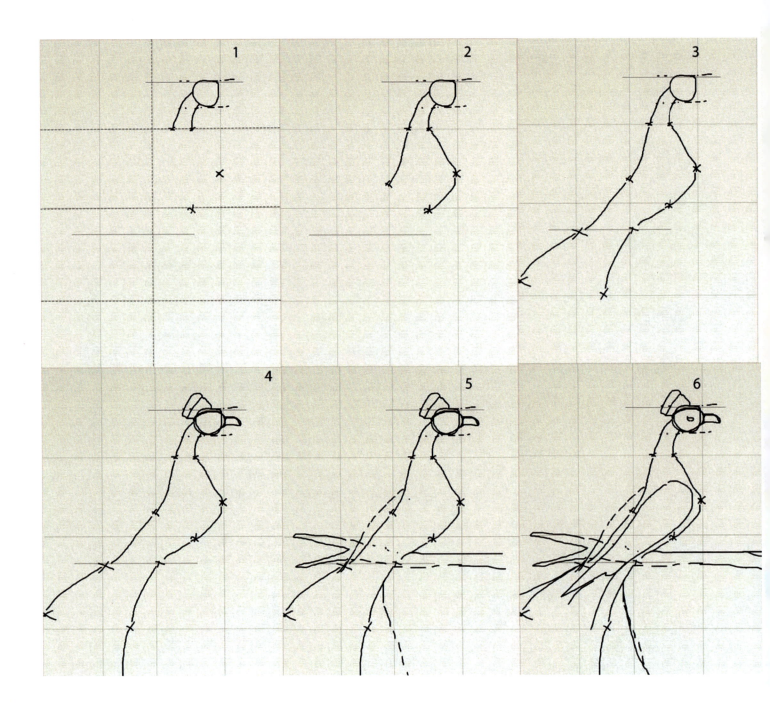

Painting Steps:

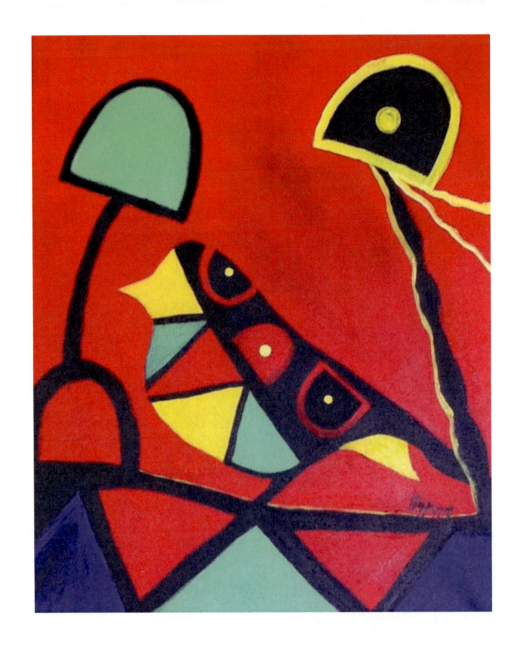

Spring Bird—Acrylic on Canvas

Colors: red, yellow, black, blue
or
cadmium red, cadmium yellow, lamp black, ultramarine blue

Colors Used:

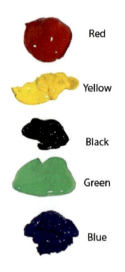

Red
Yellow
Black
Green
Blue

Grid canvas is used in this tutorial. Follow the instructions for how to prepare a grid canvas (see page 11), or skip the grid, and go straight to painting.

Using a light pencil, do your best to sketch out the bird. Make the lines faint and don't worry too much about making it perfect, because you'll go over it with paint anyway.

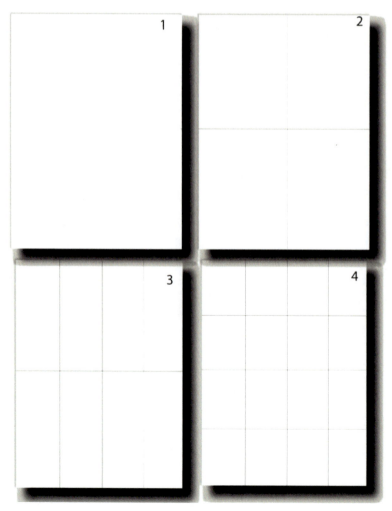

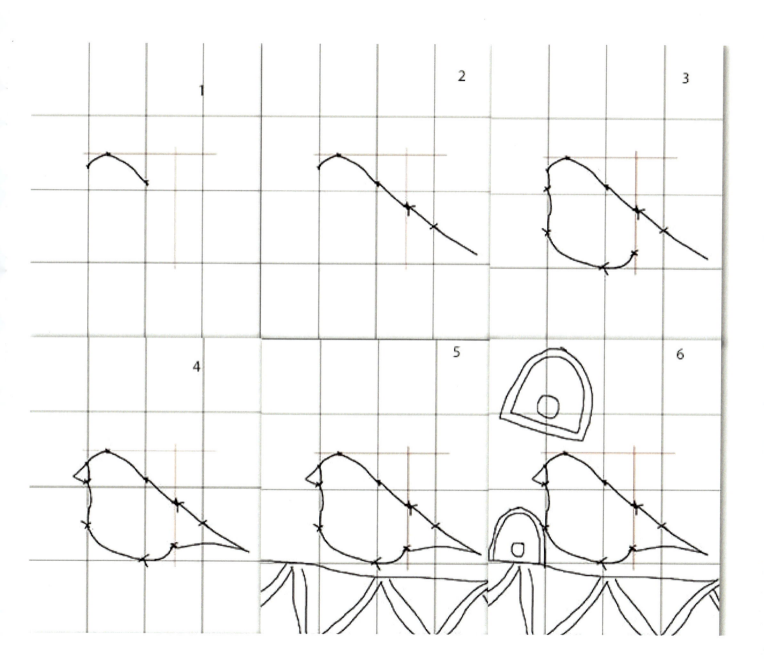

39

You do not have to add this much detail to your drawing. You can stop at stage five, and proceed to add colors. Do a detailed drawing, if you want it to be as close as possible to the original.

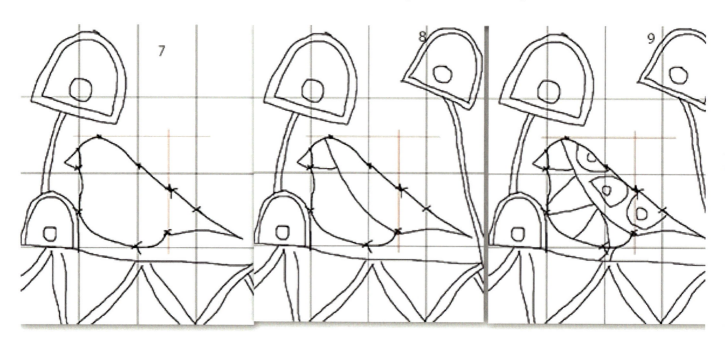

Painting Steps:

Conclusion

Hey, you did it! You created a painting of your own! Halleluiah!

Now that you have finished painting, remember to wash your brushes with cold or lukewarm water and leave them upright in a jar. Carefully dispose of your paper plates and help your host tidy up so they too can relax and take in all the beautiful works just created.

From my experience hosting paint parties, I knew you'll succeed at this and also knew you will enjoy it. I know that if you let yourself relax and not over-think this activity you will surprise yourself. I hope that happened.

Have a good rest of the party and remember to always paint whenever you need to unwind. Always choose to *sip and paint with happiness. Happiness is a brand.*

Made in the USA
Middletown, DE
17 February 2017